26.25   J 916

J 916

CULTURAL CONTRIBUTIONS FROM

AFRICA

BANJOS, COFFEE, AND MORE

GREAT CULTURES,
GREAT IDEAS

HOLLY DUHIG

PowerKiDS
press.

Published in 2019 by The Rosen Publishing Group, Inc.
29 East 21st Street, New York, NY 10010

Cataloging-in-Publication Data

Names: Duhig, Holly.
Title: Cultural contributions from Africa: banjos, coffee, and more / Holly Duhig.
Description: New York : PowerKids Press, 2019. | Series: Great cultures, great ideas | Includes glossary and index.
Identifiers: LCCN ISBN 9781538338148 (pbk.) | ISBN 9781538338131 (library bound) | ISBN 9781538338155 (6 pack)
Subjects: LCSH: Civilization, Western--African influences--Juvenile literature. | Africa--Civilization--Juvenile literature.
Classification: LCC DT14.D84 2019 | DDC 960--dc23

Written by: Holly Duhig
Edited by: Kirsty Holmes
Designed by: Gareth Liddington

Photo credits
Abbreviations: l-left, r-right, b-bottom, t-top, c-center, m-middle.

Front Cover – Konyayeva, 3DMAVR, Scorpp, Amr Hassanein, maramorosz, Pro3DArtt, 2 – Volodymyr Burdiak, 4 – stocker1970, Jakkarin Apikornrat, AJP, Memory Stockphoto, piyaphong, 5 – Sergey Clocikov, AJ Frames, Sata Production, 6 – I am Corona, hxdyl, leungchopan, 7 – Maximumvector, charnsitr, maxfoto.shutter, www.petrovvladimir.ru, 8 – Leonid Andronov, Emir Simsek, 9 – adike, Marjoli Pentz, 10 – Giovanni Dall'Orto, Peter Hermes Furian, 11 – photick, Andrea Izzotti, 12 – Evgenii Bobrov, Fedor Selivanov, 13 – WitR, Andrea Izzotti, 14 – somkhuan khanthong, 15 – thor Voronin, 16 – Ann Moore, Oleg Znamenskiy, 17 – Fotos593, Anton_Ivanov, 18 – Anton_Ivanov, Ragnar Singaas, 19 – BluesyPete, 20 – Quick Shot, Olek95, 21 – BluesyPete, 22 – VisFineArt, 23 – Rama, Igor Normann, 24 – Bobbi Joy, PRILL, maramorosz, 25 – sigiuz, Sk_Advance studio, Ola-ola, Hayati Kayhan, 26 – Anton_Ivanov, Vladimir Dvoynikov, 27 – Rob Byron, Master Video, 28 – Tyler Olson, Puwadol Jaturawutthichai, 29 – Dmitry Kalinovsky, Oldrich Barak, 30 – Ran Zisovitch

Images are courtesy of Shutterstock.com. With thanks to Getty Images, Thinkstock Photo and iStockphoto.

Manufactured in the United States of America

CPSIA Compliance Information: Batch #CSPK18: For Further Information contact Rosen Publishing, New York, New York at 1-800-237-9932.

CONTENTS

Words that look like **this** are explained in the glossary on page 31.

WHAT IS CULTURE?

If you were to travel around the world, visiting lots of countries on the way, you would probably notice that certain things around you would not be the same as they are at home. The countries and places you visit, and the people you meet, would have different languages, customs, and ways of doing things. The food might be different, the way people dress might be different, and even the laws and rules might be different to what you know at home. All of these things, when put together, make up what we call the culture of a place.

A HOUSE IN CHINA MIGHT LOOK VERY DIFFERENT THAN ONE IN THE UK!

WHAT MAKES UP A CULTURE?

Shared ideas and traditions that make up a culture can include:

LAWS	HOLIDAYS
FOOD	FAMILIES
LEADERS	SCHOOLS
SYMBOLS	SPECIAL BUILDINGS
BELIEFS	HOSPITALS
CEREMONIES	ENTERTAINMENT

A culture can also be shared by a group of people who might not live near each other, but who share a way of life. People who like the same music or hobbies can share a culture. People who all belong to the same religion can be said to share a culture, no matter where they live.

BEAUTIFUL HENNA TATTOOS ARE PART OF INDIAN CULTURE. MANY INDIAN BRIDES AROUND THE WORLD PRACTICE THIS CULTURAL TRADITION.

Our culture is a big part of our identity. Having a distinctive culture is what makes places or people unique. Knowing you belong to a particular culture is a good feeling. It's nice to share our culture with other people. If we are in a culture we recognize, we understand what to do or how to act.

DIFFERENT CULTURES GREET EACH OTHER IN DIFFERENT WAYS — A HANDSHAKE, A BOW, OR EVEN A KISS!

Even though every culture is different and unique, many cultures also have lots of things in common. We can learn a lot from other cultures, and share the things we know and like. In the past, when people started traveling to other cultures, they swapped and shared their food.

They shared traditions and knowledge, and people started to adopt things from other cultures into their own. For example, British people see drinking tea as part of their cultural identity – but tea is originally from China and is also an important part of Japanese culture.

AFTERNOON TEA, WITH CAKES AND SANDWICHES, IS A TRADITIONAL PART OF ENGLISH CULTURE.

IN JAPAN, THE TEA CEREMONY IS AN IMPORTANT CULTURAL RITUAL.

It is also really interesting to explore other cultures and discover new and exciting ways of doing things! We can share our ideas and learn new things when cultures meet.

TEA WAS ORIGINALLY FROM CHINA AND ORIGINATED DURING THE SHANG DYNASTY.

MY CULTURE, YOUR CULTURE, OUR CULTURE

Adopting ideas from other cultures can lead to really interesting results. Many cultures take inspiration from others and adapt and change their traditions and customs to make them their own. Putting two ideas from two different cultures together can produce new and exciting things. Did you know that a pizza in Italy will look very different from a pizza in the US? Italians introduced pizza, a traditional Italian dish, to the Americans living in the US. A traditional Italian pizza has a thin, crispy crust, lots of tomato but only a small amount of mozzarella cheese. An American pizza has a thick, fluffy base, is smothered in cheese and can have lots of different toppings – meats, fish, even pineapple! Both cultures share a love for pizza, but each culture has their own way of doing things!

TRADITIONAL ITALIAN PIZZA

TRADITIONAL AMERICAN PIZZA

WHICH PIZZA DO YOU PREFER? ITALIAN, AMERICAN, OR MAYBE A SLICE OF EACH?

WHERE IS AFRICA?

Africa is the second-largest continent on Earth, with 55 states recognized by the African Union. The Equator crosses Africa in the middle, meaning that half of Africa is in the Northern **Hemisphere** and half is in the Southern Hemisphere.

Ethiopia

Capital city: Addis Ababa
Population: 105,000,000 people
Size: 426,400 square miles
(1,104,370 sq km)
Currency: Birr
Major religion(s): Christianity, Islam
Main language(s): Amharic, Oromo, Tigrinya, Somali

CAIRO, EGYPT

Mali

Capital city: Bamako
Population: 18,000,000 people
Size: 478,800 square miles
(1,240,086 sq km)
Currency: CFA (Communauté Financière Africaine) franc
Major religion(s): Islam, traditional religions
Main language(s): French, Bambara, Berber, Arabic

CAN YOU SPOT WHERE AFRICA IS?

Egypt

Capital city: Cairo
Population: 98,000,000 people
Size: 390,100 square miles
(1,010,354 sq km)
Currency: Egyptian Pound
Major religion(s): Islam, Christianity
Main language(s): Arabic

South Africa

Capital city: Three capital cities: Pretoria, Cape Town, and Bloemfontain
Population: 57,000,000 people
Size: 470,900 square miles
(1,219,625 sq km)
Currency: Rand
Major religion(s): Christianity, Islam, traditional religions
Main language(s): 11 official languages including English, Afrikaans, Sesotho, Setswana, Xhosa, and Zulu

CAPE TOWN, SOUTH AFRICA

WRITING PAPER

We use paper all the time for writing, drawing, and sending letters, but did you know we have the ancient Egyptians to thank for this handy stuff? As far back as 6,000 years ago, the Egyptians were making a type of paper, called papyrus, out of the **pith** of the papyrus plant, which grew on the banks of the river Nile.

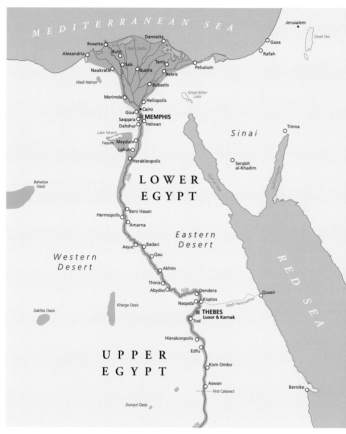

THE ENGLISH WORD "PAPER" WAS DERIVED FROM THE WORD PAPYRUS.

THESE PIECES OF PAPYRUS ARE PART OF A COLLECTION OF RELIGIOUS TEXTS AND MAGIC SPELLS CALLED "THE BOOK OF THE DEAD."

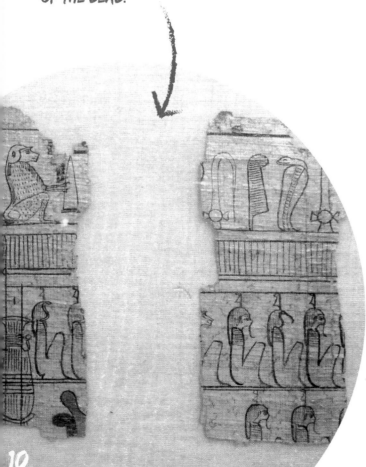

The Egyptians were a very advanced **civilization** and used papyrus to write and record what they knew about medicine, **surgery**, and mathematics. They also used it for writing down folk tales and religious beliefs. However, papyrus was far from perfect. It got damaged easily and couldn't bend without breaking. It was eventually replaced with parchment, a more flexible paper made from animal skins.

Not only did the Egyptians invent paper to write on, they also invented pens and ink to write with. Not many people knew how to write in ancient Egypt. Those who did were called scribes. Scribes made pens out of reeds by carving them into a point and making a split at the end. The split would hold on to the ink while the pen was being used. Ancient Egyptian ink was made by burning materials such as wood or oil and mixing them with water. To keep the mixture from clumping together, they used **resin** from trees, which also helped the ink to stick to the papyrus. Reed pens made large and beautiful strokes, which were ideal for writing in hieroglyphics, the ancient Egyptian **writing system**. Hieroglyphics used pictures, called hieroglyphs, instead of letters. Each picture stood for a different sound. For example, a picture of an owl was "m" and a picture of a foot stood for "b."

TREE RESIN IS A NATURAL GLUE.

REED PEN

11

HIEROGLYPHICS

Hieroglyphics are very beautiful. They can be read in any direction, from right to left, left to right, or even top to bottom. This writing system used over 1,000 different symbols. Symbols stood for single letters or whole words. Some even stood for both! A picture of an eye could mean the word "eye" or the letter "I." Historians call hieroglyphs that stand for whole words ideograms, and hieroglyphs that stand for sounds phonograms.

BECAUSE HIEROGLYPHICS WERE SO COMPLICATED, ANCIENT EGYPTIANS HAD TO TRAIN FOR YEARS TO BECOME SCRIBES.

Can you decode the hidden message on this papyrus? The answer is upside down at the bottom of page 32.

WHAT DID THE PHARAOH SAY WHEN HE SAW THE PYRAMID?

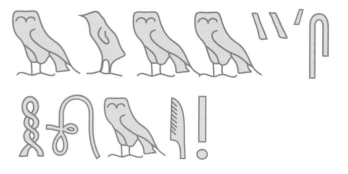

THIS IS THE HIEROGLYPHIC ALPHABET. CAN YOU WRITE YOUR NAME IN HIEROGLYPHS?

A	F	KH	K	Y
A	M	O	G	Y
IE	N	SZ	T	UW
UW	R	S	TJ	M
B	H	SH	D	N
P	H	K	DJ	L

12

PYRAMIDS

Africa also gave us one of the Seven Wonders of the Ancient World – The Great Pyramid of Giza. The many pyramids at Giza are some of Africa's most recognizable landmarks. They were originally built to be giant tombs for ancient Egyptian kings, called pharaohs. The Great Pyramid is the biggest.

Historians believe that it took 23 years and thousands of people to build. This pyramid was built for Pharaoh Khufu and, so far, we have discovered three chambers. One was a burial chamber which was to be Khufu's final resting place. The Egyptian kings certainly liked to plan ahead!

ANCIENT EGYPTIANS WASHED THEIR DEAD, REMOVED THEIR ORGANS, AND WRAPPED THEM IN CLOTH.

When ancient Egyptians died, lots of steps were taken to look after their bodies and stop them from **decaying**. This was called mummification and was important because ancient Egyptians believed that they would need their bodies in the afterlife. Mummified bodies are called mummies.

PEOPLE SOMETIMES DRESS UP AS MUMMIES FOR HALLOWEEN!

TOOTHPASTE

That's right! Toothpaste is as old as the ancient Egyptians! But back then it wasn't the minty-fresh stuff we use today. Some of the earliest Egyptian toothpaste recipes included the powder of ox hooves, burnt eggshells, and ground-down pumice, which is a type of volcanic rock. Sounds gritty!

BEFORE DENTISTS WERE AROUND TO SAVE THE DAY, PEOPLE HAD TO TAKE EXTRA GOOD CARE OF THEIR TEETH!

Later on in the Egyptian period – which stretched from around 3100 BC to 30 BC – the ingredients were much nicer and slightly more **edible**. One recipe from the 4th century AD included salt and pepper, dried iris flowers, and even mint.

Mint is a refreshing ingredient that is still used today. When modern-day dentists found the recipe, they tried it out for themselves. The recipe was still far from perfect – one dentist said it made his gums bleed!

ARCHAEOLOGISTS EVEN FOUND A GUIDE FOR BRUSHING TEETH WRITTEN ON PAPYRUS. BRUSHING MUST HAVE BEEN IMPORTANT TO THE ANCIENT EGYPTIANS.

MINT

SALT AND PEPPER

MAKEUP

Egyptians were one of the first civilizations to use makeup. They mostly wore green eyepaint, made of copper, and black kohl around their eyes. Kohl was made by grinding up soot, fatty materials, and either copper or lead metal into a paste. They also used red paint on their cheeks, and henna (a type of dye) on their hands, nails, and hair.

THE ANCIENT EGYPTIANS EVEN MADE MAKEUP BRUSHES OUT OF WOOD, IVORY, AND BONE.

EGYPTIAN MEN AND WOMEN (AND SOMETIMES CHILDREN) WORE MAKEUP.

Egyptians wore makeup because they liked the way it looked and because it helped protect their eyes from the Sun. They believed their makeup had healing powers, but they couldn't have been more wrong. Lead is poisonous to humans!

If you are exposed to lead for a long period of time, like the Egyptians were, it will affect your brain. It will give you headaches, make you angry, and cause sleep problems. It can also give you stomach cramps and, eventually, cause your kidneys to fail.

15

SAFARI

Would you like to see a lion, zebra, or even an elephant in their natural **habitat**? This is what African wildlife safaris are all about, and they are a huge tourist attraction in Africa. "Safari" is a Swahili word that means "journey" in English, so a wildlife safari literally means a journey through wildlife.

A GROUP OF LIONS IS CALLED A PRIDE.

East Africa is home to the Serengeti Plains, which are 12,000 square miles (31,079 sq km) of flat, dry grassland that span the countries of Tanzania and Kenya. The warm weather and wide open landscapes are perfect for **roaming** animals, such as lions, and the plant life provides the perfect food for **grazing** animals like giraffes. Animal lovers from all over the world go on safari vacations in Africa. Over 90,000 tourists visit the Serengeti National Park every year, and many of them go on wildlife safaris.

COFFEE

Coffee is known for the energy boost it gives its drinkers, and it is enjoyed all over the world. The drink has become an important part of the culture of the US and many other countries, such as Italy. But where did coffee start?

Coffee is made from seeds that grow inside the red berries of the coffee plant. Wild coffee plants grow in the East African country of Ethiopia, where there is a local legend about how coffee was discovered.

EVEN THOUGH WE CALL THEM BEANS, COFFEE BEANS ARE ACTUALLY SEEDS.

HUMANS AROUND THE WORLD DRINK OVER 500 BILLION CUPS OF COFFEE EVERY YEAR.

According to the legend, a goat herder named Kaldi found his goats dancing, prancing, and frolicking. He realized they had been eating red berries from a particular tree. He decided to try the berries for himself and soon became just as happy and energetic as the goats.

If the legend is true, then the reason the goats became so energetic was because the seeds of the coffee plant are naturally **caffeinated**, which means they boost your energy and your heart rate.

RUNNERS

East Africa is famous for being home to some of the best runners and athletes ever. Some of the fastest runners come from here! Running is a popular sport and hobby in countries like Ethiopia, Kenya, and Somalia. Some of these runners go on to compete at famous sporting events like the Olympics.

The famous athlete Mo Farah was born in Somalia but moved to London when he was only eight years old. Since then, he has won four Olympic gold medals.

The small village of Bekoji in Ethiopia, which is home to around 17,000 people, has produced seven Olympic medal-winning runners. One is Tirunesh Dibaba, who won three Olympic gold medals and holds the 5,000 meters track world record. She has five sisters, and two of them are Olympic silver medalists.

ExxonMobil
DIBABA
OSLO 2008

TIRUNESH DIBABA BEGAN PARTICIPATING IN ATHLETICS AT ONLY 14 YEARS OLD.

KILIMANJARO

Tanzania is home to the tallest mountain in Africa, Mount Kilimanjaro. Mount Kilimanjaro is 19,341 feet (5,895 meters) high and has three **volcanic cones**. Two of these are extinct and won't erupt again. One is only dormant, which means it hasn't erupted in a while, but might erupt again one day. People from many different countries flock to Africa to take on the challenge of climbing Kilimanjaro, and it really is a challenge!

IN 2017, THE RECORD FOR THE HIGHEST GAME OF FOOTBALL, OR SOCCER, EVER PLAYED WAS SET BY A GROUP OF 30 WOMEN ATHLETES FROM EQUAL PLAYING FIELD, A CHARITY DEDICATED TO MAKING OPPORTUNITIES EQUAL FOR WOMEN IN SPORTS.

The farther up the mountain you climb, the colder it gets, and the less **oxygen** is in the air. Temperatures at the peak can drop as low as -20°F (-29°C). The lack of oxygen can cause something called altitude sickness, which causes many travelers to have to come back down. It takes your body a long time to get used to having less oxygen, which is why most people climb Kilimanjaro very slowly over several days.

ASTRONOMY

Have you ever looked up into the night sky and done some stargazing? This was a favorite pastime of the ancient Dogon people in the West African country of Mali. The Dogon people still live in Mali today, and have their own language and traditional religions.

THE DOGON PEOPLE'S ADVANCED KNOWLEDGE HAS LED SOME PEOPLE TO BELIEVE THAT THEY WERE VISITED BY AN ALIEN RACE THOUSANDS OF YEARS AGO WHO TOLD THEM EVERYTHING THEY KNEW ABOUT THE GALAXY!

SOME PEOPLE THINK THE ANCIENT EGYPTIANS ALSO GOT THEIR KNOWLEDGE OF MATH AND ASTRONOMY FROM ALIENS. IT IS MORE LIKELY THAT THEY WERE JUST VERY CLEVER!

Hundreds of years before high-tech modern telescopes existed, the Dogon people knew about Saturn's rings, Jupiter's moons, and the fact that the Milky Way is shaped like a spiral. They even seemed to know about a whole other solar system that orbited the star Sirius. Some people think they even knew about the second star in that solar system—now called Sirius B—which is invisible to the human eye without telescopes. It is thought they figured all this out using only simple equipment!

CEREMONIAL MASKS

The Dogon people, and many other African cultures, are also famous for their art and especially for their mask-making. African ceremonial masks are designed to look like humans and animals, and sometimes a mixture of both! Mask making as an art form is a very special skill and fathers will often teach their sons how to make them.

RESPECTED DOGON PEOPLE LEARN TO CARRY EXTREMELY TALL MASKS IN THEIR TEETH!

AFRICAN MASKS HAVE INFLUENCED ART AND ARTISTS ALL OVER THE WORLD, INCLUDING THE FAMOUS SPANISH ARTIST PICASSO.

Masks are usually made from wood and are decorated using all sorts of natural materials such as paint, seashells, feathers, grass, animal hair, and animal teeth. Masks hold special **symbolism** and are often used in religious **worship** and dancing ceremonies. The Dogon people hold dancing ceremonies to honour their **ancestors**. These can last for three whole days.

PHOTOCOPY OR TRACE
THIS PAGE SO OTHER
PEOPLE WHO READ THIS
BOOK CAN TRY IT, TOO!

Ceremonial masks are
a traditional art form
in many countries
and cultures all
over Africa. Each
of these cultures
have their own
traditional styles.

1: Don't forget
to cut out the
eye holes on
your mask!

2: The red dots
show where to
make holes in your
mask. You can use
these holes to tie
string to your mask
so you can wear it.

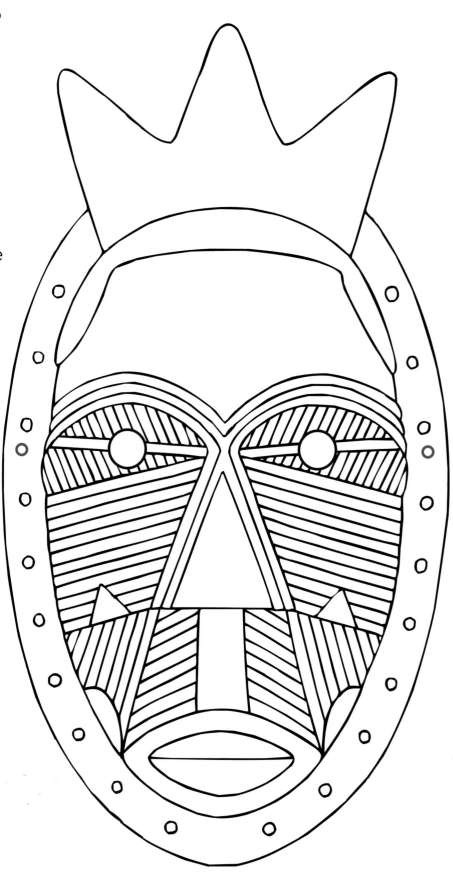

SCULPTURE

There is also a long tradition of sculpture making in West Africa. In Nigeria, sculptures are made to look like people, but often with **elongated** faces, bodies, arms, and legs, which can look very elegant.

The tradition of sculpture making is an old one. Some of the earliest African sculptures were made by an Iron Age culture called the Nok culture in the country of Nigeria. These sculptures were made of terra-cotta.

Other ancient sculptures were found in Nigeria in the ancient city of Ife. These were thought to be made to look like real people and were made of metals such as copper.

DRUMS

As well as art, West Africa is known for its music and the **percussion** instruments that they use to make it.

THE TALKING DRUM

The talking drum is shaped like an **hourglass** and is designed to sound like human speech when played. It was first used in Nigeria as a way of communicating to different **tribes** over long distances.

THE DJEMBE

The djembe is a type of drum first made by the Mandinke tribe, who lived in Mali in the 12th century. The base of the drum is traditionally made from a hollowed out tree trunk, and the top is made from goat's skin. Many traditional drums were made this way. This is why even though most modern drums are made out of plastic we still call the top of a drum its "skin."

THE BANJO ALSO COMES FROM WEST AFRICA. EARLY BANJOS WERE HOLLOWED GOURDS WITH STRINGS.

HOW TO PLAY A DJEMBE

Three main sounds can be played on a djembe. These are called a bass, tone, and slap.

BASS

A bass is a low-pitched sound played by hitting the drum in the middle with a heavy hand.

TONE

A tone is a sound somewhere between a bass and slap in pitch. It is played by hitting the edge of the drum, using the arm and wrist to give the hand more force.

SLAP

The slap sound is also played near the edge of the drum but slightly nearer to the middle than the tone. The slap is the highest-pitched sound and is the hardest stroke to achieve.

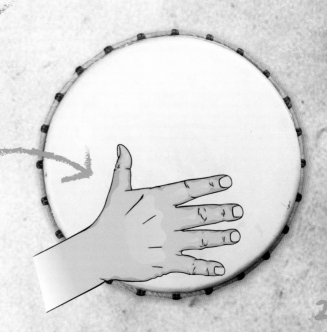

25

VOODOO RELIGION

Voodoo is a religion that has its roots in the West-African country Benin. It focuses on the spirits of ancestors, nature, and animals, and its followers believe that the world of the living and the world of the dead are closely linked together.

You may have heard of voodoo from TV, books, and movies. Maybe you've seen the classic voodoo doll with pins through its eyes, or heard of voodoo magic and hexes.

All of this makes for a good scary story, but this isn't what voodoo is actually about. This religion is about paying respect to nature and remembering ancestors.

STORIES OF WITCHCRAFT AND MAGIC SPELLS IN EUROPE HAVE BEEN INSPIRED BY VOODOO CULTURE IN WEST AFRICA.

Have you ever watched a scary movie where someone is possessed by an evil spirit? This idea also has its roots in voodoo. Followers believe the dead can communicate with the living by temporarily taking over, or "possessing," someone's body. However, in voodoo, these are usually good spirits who want to help.

THESE WOMEN ARE CELEBRATING THE VOODOO FESTIVAL IN BENIN, AFRICA.

SURGICAL ROBOTS

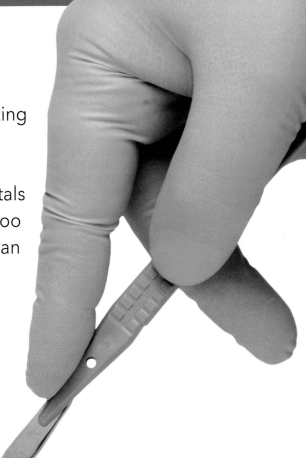

From ancient sculptures to some of the most cutting-edge technology of today, Africa has it all. In the country of South Africa, many amazing medical advances are being used. Possibly the most futuristic of these is the da Vinci surgical robot. This is a robot that can be used in hospitals to help surgeons perform operations that are too delicate for human hands. The da Vinci robot can be controlled by trained surgeons from over 1,180 miles (1,900 km) away. This means that if you were to need an operation, the surgeon wouldn't even have to be in the same hospital while they are operating on you!

IMAGINE BEING STITCHED BACK TOGETHER BY TINY ROBOT ARMS!

THIS ROBOT IS ABLE TO USE SMALL SURGICAL INSTRUMENTS LIKE SCALPELS.

The technology isn't perfect yet. There is still a slight delay between the surgeon telling the robot what to do and the robot doing it. Surgeons have to react quickly if anything goes wrong, so it might be a while before surgical robots become common.

CT SCANS

Another piece of medical technology South Africa has given the world is the CT scan. CT stands for computerized tomography, and unlike the da Vinci robot, this is already being used in hospitals all over the world. CT scans use x-rays and a computer to build up a detailed picture of the inside of a patient's body.

These have helped save many lives by detecting diseases such as cancer. A CT scanner has a large ring that rotates around one section of your body at a time as you pass through it. Unlike other body scanners, the CT doesn't surround a patient's whole body at once, which makes the scan much more comfortable.

CT SCANS ALLOW DOCTORS TO LOOK AT A PARTICULAR PART OR CROSS SECTION OF A PATIENT'S BODY.

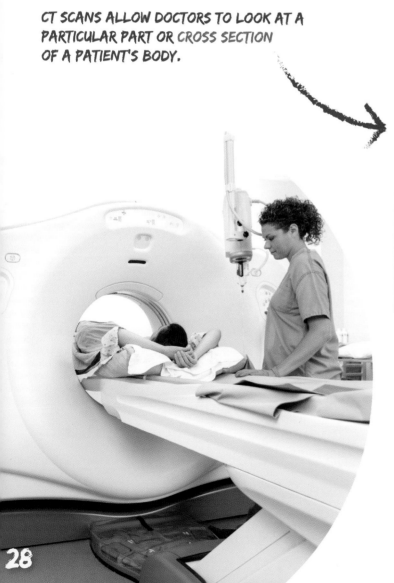

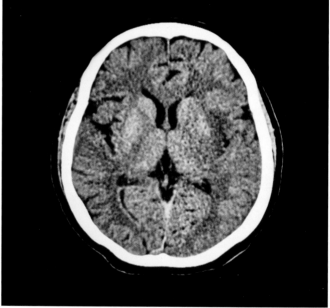

Allan McLeod Cormack was a South African American physicist who was born in Johannesburg in South Africa. He worked with British physicist Godfrey Hounsfield to invent the CT scanner. Both men shared the Nobel Prize for their invention.

HEART TRANSPLANT

Possibly the most difficult operation doctors can perform is a heart transplant, which is where a surgeon removes a patient's unhealthy heart and replaces it with a healthy one. They are risky because we need our hearts to be working extra hard to keep us alive while an operation is taking place. After all, humans can't live without their hearts for very long.

THE FIRST PATIENT TO RECEIVE A HEART TRANSPLANT WAS LOUIS WASHKANSKY, AND HIS OPERATION TOOK SIX HOURS!

The world's first successful heart transplant was performed by the South African doctor Christiaan Barnard. Because of the difficulty of operating on a beating heart, Dr. Barnard used a heart-lung machine during the surgery. This machine temporarily does the job of the heart and lungs by pumping blood and making sure the body has plenty of oxygen. Surgeons still use a heart-lung machine when operating on the heart today.

POTJIEKOS

In South Africa, it is traditional to cook food in pots called potjie (pronounced poi-key) pots. These are big, iron pots that look like witches' cauldrons and are used on an open fire. The meals that are cooked in these pots are called potjiekos (pronounced poi-key-cos), and they are often cooked and served outside where they can be cooked on a fire. Potjiekos meals are left to cook and soften for a long time to draw all the flavors out of the ingredients. This type of cooking is called slow cooking.

POTJIE POTS CAME ABOUT BECAUSE THEY WERE USEFUL FOR FEEDING BIG GROUPS OF PEOPLE.

Slow cooking is now popular worldwide. The electronic slow cooker, or Crock-pot, is popular around the world. Its design is based on potjie pots.

MANY SOUTH AFRICAN PEOPLE WILL START COOKING A POTJIEKOS MEAL A WHOLE DAY BEFORE EATING IT!

GLOSSARY

ancestors   persons from whom one is descended, such as a great-grandparent

archaeologists   historians who study buried ruins and ancient objects in order to learn about human history

caffeinated   containing caffeine; a natural stimulant

civilization   a society that is very advanced

cross section   a view into the inside of something made by cutting through it

decaying   to rot or decompose

edible   safe to be eaten

elongated   stretched out or made longer

grazing   eating a lot of plants for nutrients

habitat   the natural environment in which animals or plants live

hemisphere   a section of the Earth, either Northern, Southern, Eastern, or Western

hourglass   a shape that is wider at the top and bottom than in the middle

organs   parts of the body that have their own specific jobs or functions

oxygen   a natural gas that all living things need in order to survive

percussion   a family of instruments that are played by hitting their surfaces with a hand or object

pith   spongy tissue found in the stems of plants

resin   a gummy substance made by trees

roaming   wandering freely or aimlessly, often over a wide area

surgery   medical treatments that involve operating on the body and cutting into it

symbolism   when a thing represents something else, usually a physical object that represents something nonphysical

tribes   groups of people linked together by family, culture, religion, or community

volcanic cones   triangle-shaped hills created by volcanic eruptions

worship   a religious act where a person expresses their love for a god or gods

writing system   any method of representing the sounds of a language in written symbols

INDEX